God's Will, Our Initiative

Lessons from the Parable of the Talents

Dale S. Schultz

Beech Hill Press

GOD'S WILL, OUR INITIATIVE
Copyright © 2009 by Dale S. Schultz

All Scripture quotations are from the New International Version, © 1973, 1978, 1984 by International Bible Society.

All rights reserved. No part of this document may be reproduced, distributed, or transmitted in any form or by any means, or stored in a database or retrieval system, without the prior written permission of the author.

Cover art includes a reproduction of a Woodcut from *Historiae celebriores Veteris Testamenti Iconibus representatae,* 1712, a work of public domain.

ISBN: 978-0-615-34443-0

Published by
Beech Hill Press
85 Beech Hill Drive
Newark, Delaware 19711
USA

For information, visit our web site,
www.BeechHillPress.com
or send email to info@BeechHillPress.com

To our great and loving heavenly Master
who graciously provides his children
the means and opportunities
to build His kingdom

God's Will, Our Initiative

The Parable		i
Chapter One	TALENTS	1
Chapter Two	DESTINY	10
Chapter Three	GOD'S WILL	22
Chapter Four	PROVIDENCE	42
Chapter Five	WISDOM	59
Chapter Six	INITIATIVE	77
Chapter Seven	MISSION	93
Epilogue	GOD'S PRESENCE	99

The Parable

Matthew 25:14-30

Again, it will be like a man going on a journey, who called his servants and entrusted his property to them.

- To one he gave five talents of money,
- to another two talents, and
- to another one talent,

each according to his ability. Then he went on his journey.

The man who had received the five talents went at once and put his money to work and gained five more.

So also, the one with the two talents gained two more.

But the man who had received the one talent went off, dug a hole in the ground and hid his master's money.

After a long time the master of those servants returned and settled accounts with them.

The man who had received the five talents brought the other five. "Master," he said, "you entrusted me with five talents. See, I have gained five more." His master replied, "Well done, good and faithful servant! You have been faithful with a few things;

I will put you in charge of many things. Come and share your master's happiness!"

The man with the two talents also came. "Master," he said, "you entrusted me with two talents; see, I have gained two more." His master replied, "Well done, good and faithful servant! You have been faithful with a few things; I will put you in charge of many things. Come and share your master's happiness!"

Then the man who had received the one talent came. "Master," he said, "I knew that you are a hard man, harvesting where you have not sown and gathering where you have not scattered seed. So I was afraid and went out and hid your talent in the ground. See, here is what belongs to you."

His master replied, "You wicked, lazy servant! So you knew that I harvest where I have not sown and gather where I have not scattered seed? Well then, you should have put my money on deposit with the bankers, so that when I returned I would have received it back with interest.

"Take the talent from him and give it to the one who has the ten talents. For everyone who has will be given more, and he will have an abundance. Whoever does not have, even what he has will be taken from him. And throw that worthless servant outside, into the darkness, where there will be weeping and gnashing of teeth."

1

Talents

Jesus' story known as the Parable of the Talents has had an enduring impact in the lives of believers. As one of the final three parables recorded in the book of Matthew, it is part of Jesus' response to his disciples' questions about signs of "the end of the age." He warns of wars, famines, earthquakes, persecutions, death, betrayal, and false prophets – and also proclaims that the "gospel of the kingdom will be preached in the whole world" (Matthew 24:6-14). These parables teach about the coming of that kingdom and the role believers have in building it.

The Parable of the Talents is compelling because though simple, it touches on many fundamental aspects of the believer's life. These include issues of destiny and choice, understanding God's will, the nature of God's providence, our need to gain and apply wisdom in daily decisions, and our responsibility to exercise initiative in building God's kingdom.

The Parable tells of the conduct of three servants during their master's absence and how the master responds when he returns. As he left on his journey, the master gave either five, two, or one talent of money to each. The first two servants immediately put the money to work and ultimately doubled their investment, but the third servant merely dug a hole and hid his talent. Upon his return, the master summoned the servants to settle accounts with them. When the two faithful servants presented their earnings, they were invited to celebrate with the master and told that they would be given more responsibility. When the third servant returned his talent, he was chastised for being lazy and worthless, and was banished from the master's presence.

    The parallel between the master entrusting money to his servants and God entrusting skills and abilities to humans is so strong that it has transformed the very meaning of the word "talent". In Jesus' day, a talent was a measure of weight or of monetary currency. If not for this story, the word probably would have fallen out of use long ago. That we still use the word "talent" testifies to the power of this story and what it has to teach about how God wants us to live.

****

    This book explores the meaning of the Parable of the Talents in terms of five major themes: Destiny, God's Will, Providence, Wisdom, and Initiative. These themes are briefly introduced below. In subsequent chapters each is addressed in more detail within a broader context of Scripture.

Destiny   The master was certain to return and hold his servants accountable.

God's Will   The good results the master desired were clearly understood by his servants.

Providence   The servants were provided the resources needed to fulfill their responsibilities.

Wisdom   Accomplishing their mission required the servants to be wise in making decisions.

Initiative   The servants were not given specific plans, so it was necessary that they exercise initiative.

Destiny

None of the servants doubted that the master would return and hold him accountable for his actions. We apply this principle to our lives by asking: *What will God hold me accountable for?*

Scripture is clear that when we die, we will be required to give an account of our lives.

God's Will, Our Initiative

> *For we must all appear before the judgment seat of Christ, that each one may receive what is due him for the things done while in the body, whether good or bad.*
> 2 Corinthians 5:10

The things we have done, both honorable and evil, will be evaluated according to the standard of God's moral will. And Jesus makes plain that nothing will be too small to escape notice when we are called before God to "settle accounts".

> *But I tell you that men will have to give account on the day of judgment for every careless word they have spoken.*
> Matthew 12:36

The servants did not know when their master would return from his journey, but they knew that when he did, he would settle accounts with them. Likewise, we do not know when our day of judgment will be, but it is certain to occur and the evaluation we receive will be comprehensive and thorough.

How have you prepared yourself for God's evaluation of your life?

God's Will

The master desired good results, which were clearly understood by his servants. And so we ask: *What does God expect from me?*

Talents

In the Sermon on the Mount, Jesus succinctly answers this question by expressing the priorities that are to be reflected in how we live:

> *But seek first his kingdom and his righteousness, and all these things will be given you as well.*
> Matthew 6:33

What does Jesus say should be our primary concerns? To obey God's moral law ("his righteousness") and to actively participate in building God's kingdom. This is God's will for our lives. Jesus goes on to say that all the other things we are prone to worry about pale in comparison to the satisfaction we receive by living in faithfulness to God.

Are you carrying out God's will by obeying his moral law and working to build his kingdom?

Providence

The servants were provided the resources needed to fulfill their responsibilities. *Do I have talents God has entrusted to me?*

The master entrusted one, two, or five talents to his servants, "each according to his ability" (Matthew 25:15). Likewise, Christ has equipped every believer with means to contribute to his kingdom.

God's Will, Our Initiative

> But to each one of us grace has been given as Christ has apportioned it ... so that the body of Christ may be built up until we all reach unity in the faith and in the knowledge of the Son of God and become mature, attaining to the whole measure of the fullness of Christ.
> *(from Ephesians 4:7-13)*

Building God's kingdom is required of all believers. This passage affirms that every believer is to contribute, for "to each one of us grace has been given ...". The third servant's poor performance was not due to inability, but to his failing even to try to employ the talent entrusted to him.

How are you applying your talents?

Wisdom

Accomplishing their mission required the servants to be wise in making decisions. *What role does wisdom play in the Christian life?*

> Be very careful, then, how you live – not as unwise but as wise, making the most of every opportunity, because the days are evil.
> *Ephesians 5:15-16*

This passage instructs us to apply wisdom so as to make the most of every opportunity. What kind of opportunities? Any means to glorify God and extend his kingdom. The implication is that there is no shortage of opportunities – if we apply wisdom. To make the most of every opportunity is a tall order. No wonder so much of Scripture exhorts us to gain wisdom and live by it.

> *Wisdom is supreme; therefore get wisdom.*
> *Though it cost all you have, get understanding.*
> *Proverbs 4:7*

Are you developing the wisdom required to make the most of every opportunity?

Initiative

The servants were not given specific plans, so it was necessary that they exercise initiative. *Do I have freedom to choose how I serve God?*

Too often we complain about the limitations which narrow our choices instead of being grateful for the abundance of opportunities from which we are free to choose. In his first letter to the Corinthians, the Apostle Paul teaches about the freedom believers have in making choices among morally permissible alternatives, concluding with this statement:

> *So whether you eat or drink or whatever you do, do it all for the glory of God.*
> *1 Corinthians 10:31*

God's Will, Our Initiative

The master did not tell his servants exactly how to utilize their talents, though we may assume he established appropriate boundaries within which they were to conduct themselves. Likewise, the choices I make must be consistent with God's moral will and the wisdom I gain from Scripture and other means (including my own trials and errors). But if I wait for instructions from God as to particular actions he wants – instead of taking the initiative to choose from among available opportunities – am I not like the servant who hid his talent? He deserved to be punished for his laziness. With freedom comes responsibility.

Do you appreciate the freedom God has given you to serve him?

****

Our Destiny includes being held *accountable* for our lives and receiving *rewards* for faithfulness.

God's Will is that we obey his moral law and perform good works.

By God's Providence, we have the *ability* to contribute to building his kingdom.

Applying Wisdom gained through Scripture and experience, we exercise Initiative to *create* and *choose* opportunities of service.

This is how God builds his kingdom.

Questions for Discussion and Application

- Think about what enabled the first two servants to be worthy of more than one talent. How important is past experience relative to innate ability in equipping us to be effective?

- Might the faithful servants' past experience have included failure, from which they learned lessons that enabled them to be productive? How have you learned from past failures?

- The master condemned the third servant not for failing to produce a profit, but for being lazy. What does this teach us about how God wants us to live?

****

- What talents has God entrusted to me? How am I actively developing them and applying them?

- Have I been guilty of laziness in applying my talents to build God's kingdom?

- What should I be doing to prepare for the evaluation I will receive on the Day of Judgment?

2

Destiny

Belief in some kind of fate or destiny has always fascinated the human mind. In one way or another, perhaps every mythology, religion, or philosophy has addressed the tension between fate and choice, and it continues to find expression in popular culture again and again.

In the Parable, the servants knew that the master would return to "settle accounts" with them, which is to say that the master would hold his servants responsible for how they had used the resources entrusted to them. The master had the authority, power, and intention to judge the servants and punish or reward them according to their performance. From other teachings in the New Testament, we see that this is a picture of what awaits each of us at the end of our lives, for "man is destined to die once, and after that to face judgment" (Hebrews 9:27).

The theme of destiny in the Parable focuses on the judgment the servants are to receive upon the master's return. However, the Bible teaches about many events in the history of God's interaction with his people as having been predestined to occur. We will now consider the broader theme of destiny in Scripture to prepare us for examining what is taught about the Day of Judgment we each will face.

The Sovereignty of God

Destiny as a biblical principle is rooted in the doctrine of God's sovereignty. It is by his sovereign power that he can determine in advance whatever he chooses to happen.

Sovereignty is the quality of supreme rank, power, or authority. When describing humans or human institutions, the context is key to understanding what is meant. For example, referring to a country as a "sovereign nation" does not imply that it is the most powerful of all nations, but rather that within its borders, its government is the highest authority and other nations have no right to interfere with that authority except perhaps in extreme circumstances.

However, when we speak of God's sovereignty, there are no limits. God's sovereignty is absolute. In 1 Chronicles 29:11-12 we read that that "*everything in heaven and earth*" is God's, that God is "exalted as head over *all*," and that he is the "ruler of *all* things" (emphasis added).

Deuteronomy 3:24 poses a rhetorical question to drive home the message that nothing can compare with God's sovereign power:

> *O Sovereign LORD, you have begun to show to your servant your greatness and your strong hand. For what god is there in heaven or on earth who can do the deeds and mighty works you do?*

Perhaps the best definition of God's sovereignty is found in the passages that declare God as doing whatever he pleases, as in Psalm 115:3,

> *Our God is in heaven;*
> *he does whatever pleases him.*

Similar phrases are found elsewhere (e.g., Daniel 4:35 and Proverbs 21:1). God does whatever he pleases. He is able to because his power is absolutely supreme.

Scripture's claim of God's absolute sovereignty could not be clearer. Therefore we are assured that whatever he has determined to do is destined to occur.

God's Sovereignty in Action

Starting with its very first verse, the Bible presents one demonstration after another of God's sovereignty. Many of these involve fulfillment of a prophecy, in other words, fulfillment of destiny. In

Destiny

this section, we will consider some examples from redemptive history of how God's sovereign prerogative to predetermine events was (or will be) put into effect. Various Christian traditions differ with respect to their views of the extent to which destiny governs our lives – that is, how much God chooses to control – but these Scriptures clearly demonstrate that God controls everything that he chooses to.

- God will bless all peoples on earth through Abraham

    > *I will make you into a great nation*
    > *and I will bless you;*
    > *I will make your name great,*
    > *and you will be a blessing.*
    > *Genesis 12:2*

- God will deliver his people out of Egypt

    > *And now the cry of the Israelites has reached me, and I have seen the way the Egyptians are oppressing them. So now, go. I am sending you to Pharaoh to bring my people the Israelites out of Egypt.*
    > *Exodus 3:9-10*

- The Messiah will come

    > *Therefore the Lord himself will give you a sign:*

God's Will, Our Initiative

> *The virgin will be with child and will give birth to a son, and will call him Immanuel.*
>
> Isaiah 7:14

- Jesus will be rejected by Israel

> *Indeed Herod and Pontius Pilate met together with the Gentiles and the people of Israel in this city to conspire against your holy servant Jesus, whom you anointed. They did what your power and will had decided beforehand should happen.*
>
> Acts 4:27-28

- Jesus will die a shameful death

> *This man was handed over to you by God's set purpose and foreknowledge; and you, with the help of wicked men, put him to death by nailing him to the cross.*
>
> Acts 2:23

- God's chosen people will be saved through faith in Jesus

> *In him we were also chosen, having been predestined according to the plan of him who works out everything in conformity with the purpose of his will ...*
>
> Ephesians 1:11

- All of God's chosen will be glorified

> *And we know that in all things God works for the good of those who love him, who have*

> been called according to his purpose. For those God foreknew he also predestined to be conformed to the likeness of his Son, that he might be the firstborn among many brothers. And those he predestined, he also called; those he called, he also justified; those he justified, he also glorified.
> Romans 8:28-30

- The church and its testimony will prevail

> Simon Peter answered, "You are the Christ, the Son of the living God." Jesus replied, "Blessed are you, Simon son of Jonah, for this was not revealed to you by man, but by my Father in heaven. And I tell you that you are Peter, and on this rock I will build my church, and the gates of Hades will not overcome it.
> Matthew 16:16-18

To this list, many other events that God has destined to occur could be added – including the Day of Judgment. Since this event is represented in the Parable, we will now examine it in greater detail.

Judgment Day

The Parable describes the master's return to "settle accounts" with his servants, when he judged their works. Earlier in the Book of Matthew, Jesus uses similar language to describe the final judgment that awaits each of us:

God's Will, Our Initiative

> *But I tell you that men will have to give account on the day of judgment for every careless word they have spoken.*
> Matthew 12:36

Jesus' words should make us pause and consider the level of detail in our lives for which we are accountable to God. If every careless word is to be judged against us, then nothing is too small to be considered insignificant.

Though these are words of warning, Jesus also taught about the coming day of judgment in positive terms, as when telling his followers to "store up for yourselves treasures in heaven" (Matthew 6:20). So also, Paul speaks of the day of judgment both positively and negatively:

> *For we must all appear before the judgment seat of Christ, that each one may receive what is due him for the things done while in the body, whether good or bad.*
> 2 Corinthians 5:10

From the context, we know that the judgment Paul is speaking of is not about salvation, for he is addressing this teaching to Christians. This point is made more clearly when Paul uses a building and its materials of construction as a metaphor for our works and how our lives will be judged:

> [11]*For no one can lay any foundation other than the one already laid, which is Jesus Christ.*

Destiny

> ¹²*If any man builds on this foundation using gold, silver, costly stones, wood, hay or straw, ¹³his work will be shown for what it is, because the Day will bring it to light. It will be revealed with fire, and the fire will test the quality of each man's work.*
>
> ¹⁴*If what he has built survives, he will receive his reward.*
>
> ¹⁵*If it is burned up, he will suffer loss; he himself will be saved, but only as one escaping through the flames.*
>
> 1 Corinthians 3:11-15

Paul likens the kingdom of God to a building constructed upon a solid foundation (v. 11). Our works in God's service are represented as the materials used for the structures built on the foundation. The judgment that awaits us is as a fire of testing (v. 13). One who builds with materials that survive that test, namely "gold, silver, costly stones" (v. 12) is rewarded (v. 14), but whoever builds with "wood, hay, or straw" (v. 12), will "suffer loss" (v. 15).

How do we know that the judgment Paul is describing is not about salvation? The final portion of verse 15 says that the one whose work is unsatisfactory is still saved. The "loss" suffered by such a believer is not loss of salvation, but of the rewards he could have received had his works proved effective in building God's kingdom.

Likewise, the good works depicted as gold, silver, and costly stones are not works that merit salvation. We know this must be so, for Isaiah declares our best works to be as "filthy rags" when it comes to atoning for our sin (Isaiah 64:6). Our good works are inadequate to satisfy God's holiness. Only Jesus' righteousness meets the standard of God's holiness, so it is only by having his righteousness imputed to us – by faith in Jesus – that we can be reconciled to God (Romans 3:22-24).

Yet while our good works cannot earn us salvation, they are very, very, important. This is precisely the teaching of Ephesians 2:8-10,

> *For it is by grace you have been saved, through faith – and this not from yourselves, it is the gift of God – not by works, so that no one can boast.*
>
> *For we are God's workmanship, created in Christ Jesus to do good works, which God prepared in advance for us to do.*

Our good works do not save us. They can't because they are not good enough. We are saved through faith in Jesus – faith that God in his grace gives as a gift. But this does not mean that our good works don't matter. Our ability to serve God by good works – the result of his "workmanship" in our lives – are the means God uses to build his kingdom.

Destiny

This is why we are instructed to "spur one another on to love and good deeds" (Hebrews 10:24). It is why Peter warns us to keep from "being ineffective and unproductive" (2 Peter 1:8). It is why James teaches that "faith without deeds is dead" (James 2:26) and that one who is wise will "show it by his good life, by deeds done in the humility that comes from wisdom" (James 3:13). Christians who fail to utilize their resources to build God's kingdom are still saved from punishment for their sin, but will not receive the rewards of those whose works are effective in God's service.

The faithful servants in the Parable had no cause to fear the return of the master, for they had prepared for being judged by diligently dedicating themselves to the master's work. No doubt they were eager for the master to return and hear him say, "Well done, good and faithful servant! ... Come and share your master's happiness!" Like Paul, they were motivated to work hard to "win the prize" of the master's favor:

> Not that I have already obtained all this, or have already been made perfect, but I press on to take hold of that for which Christ Jesus took hold of me.
> Brothers, I do not consider myself yet to have taken hold of it. But one thing I do: Forgetting what is behind and straining toward what is ahead, I press on toward the goal to win the prize for

which God has called me heavenward in Christ Jesus.
Philippians 3:12-14

Our day of judgment need not be something we fear. We will joyfully anticipate it – if we have diligently prepared for it by obeying God's moral law and by applying the resources entrusted to us to build his kingdom.

****

Questions for Discussion and Application

- If good works cannot merit salvation, why will God judge us according to our works?

- What are some examples of "good works" that will be rewarded?

- Why do many Christians so rarely think about God judging us on the basis of our works?

****

- How often do I think about the fact that at the end of my life God will judge me?

- What changes would I make if I lived fully aware that I will give account on the day of judgment for every careless word I have spoken?

Destiny

- How would I live differently if I truly realized that I will be rewarded for everything I have done to build God's kingdom?

- Do I fear God's judgment, or do I joyfully anticipate the rewards I will receive?

3

God's Will

The master desired good results, which were clearly understood by his servants. Our response should be to ask, "What does God expect of me?" Or, we might express it as, "What is God's will for my life?"

It is hard to imagine a Christian who has not asked these questions. But, sadly, it is all too common for believers to feel that they do not have the answers they need to live with a true sense of mission or purpose. Perhaps more than any other theme of the Parable, the theme of God's Will immediately grabs our attention.

We will begin addressing these issues by recognizing that the Bible speaks of God's will in at least two ways. Deuteronomy 29:29 offers insight into this by making a distinction between "secret things" and "things revealed":

> *The secret things belong to the LORD our God, but the things revealed belong to us and to our children forever, that we may follow all the words of this law.*

God's Will

The "secret things" are things that we do not need to know in order to serve God, and he has chosen not to make them known to us. Many aspects of his plan for ruling over his creation fall into this category. We will refer to this part of God's will as his *sovereign* will. In addition to these "secret things", there are elements of his sovereign will that God has chosen to reveal in his word, and some of these were discussed in the previous chapter.

The verse also speaks of "things revealed" for the purpose that we may obey God's law. This is God's *moral* will, which has been completely revealed in his word. God's moral will is expressed in the Ten Commandments and expanded upon extensively throughout Scripture.

In addition to God's sovereign will and his moral will, there is a third manner in which many Christians use the term "God's will". They want to know what is God's will for me as a unique individual. They are asking questions such as, "Where should I go to school and what should I study?", "What career should I pursue?", "Where should I live?", "Whom should I marry?", and so on. When we asked such questions, it may be said that we wonder about God's *individual* will for each of us.[1]

---

[1] See Garry Friesen, <u>Decision Making & the Will of God</u> (Multnomah) for a fuller discussion of the distinctions between God's sovereign will, God's moral will, and God's individual will.

With this in mind, this chapter is divided into three sections for addressing the issues related to understanding God's will:

- God's Sovereign Will
  – God's plan for ruling over all his creation

- God's Moral Will
  – God's revealed commands that teach what to believe and how to live

- Decision Making
  – How to choose among opportunities within God's moral will

God's Sovereign Will

The previous chapter laid the groundwork for understanding what we mean by the term "God's sovereign will", though that term was not used at the time. We saw that the Bible clearly teaches God's absolute sovereignty, both by explicit declaration and by example. Consider these passages that make mention of God's "will" in the sense of his sovereign will:

- Revelation 4:11
  You are worthy, our Lord and God,
  to receive glory and honor and power,
  for you created all things,
  and by your will they were created
  and have their being.

- Ephesians 1:11
    In him we were also chosen, having been predestined according to the plan of him who works out everything in conformity with the purpose of his will ...

- Romans 9:18-19
    Therefore God has mercy on whom he wants to have mercy, and he hardens whom he wants to harden.
    One of you will say to me: 'Then why does God still blame us? For who resists his will?"

Each of these texts speaks of purposes or activities God engages in for his own glory, which he will bring about no matter what. His sovereign power ensures that such things are accomplished.

God's Moral Will

Although God's sovereign will is largely unknown to us, God's moral will – his standards for our beliefs and behavior – is fully revealed in the Bible. And while God ultimately is responsible for seeing that his sovereign will is fulfilled, he places upon us responsibility for obeying his moral will. The following passages speak of God's "will" from the perspective of his moral will:

God's Will, Our Initiative

- 1 Thessalonians 5:18
  ... give thanks in all circumstances, for this is God's will for you in Christ Jesus.

- 1 Thessalonians 4:3
  It is God's will that you should be sanctified: that you should avoid sexual immorality ...

- Colossians 1:9
  For this reason, since the day we heard about you, we have not stopped praying for you and asking God to fill you with the knowledge of his will through all spiritual wisdom and understanding.

- Colossians 4:12
  Epaphras, who is one of you and a servant of Christ Jesus, sends greetings. He is always wrestling in prayer for you, that you may stand firm in all the will of God, mature and fully assured.

- Romans 12:2
  Do not conform any longer to the pattern of this world, but be transformed by the renewing of your mind. Then you will be able to test and approve what God's will is – his good, pleasing and perfect will.

- Ephesians 5:15-21
  Be very careful, then, how you live – not as unwise but as wise, making the most of every opportunity, because the days are evil. Therefore do not be foolish, but understand what the Lord's will is. Do not

God's Will

> *get drunk on wine, which leads to debauchery. Instead, be filled with the Spirit. Speak to one another with psalms, hymns and spiritual songs. Sing and make music in your heart to the Lord, always giving thanks to God the Father for everything, in the name of our Lord Jesus Christ. Submit to one another out of reverence for Christ.*

We learn from these passages that God's moral will touches upon every aspect of our lives and that it is more than just a matter of outward obedience. We are told that it is God's will that we be thankful, wise, and mature – and that as our minds are renewed and transformed, we come to see God's will as good, pleasing, and perfect.

God wants us to focus more on obeying his moral law than on any other decisions we make. Jesus made plain what our first priorities are to be when he told his followers to "seek first his kingdom and his righteousness" (Matthew 6:33). Paul told the Corinthians, "Keeping God's commands is what counts" (1 Corinthians 7:19). And Solomon summed up all the wisdom he had gained throughout his lifetime with the conclusion presented in Ecclesiastes:

> *Now all has been heard;*
> *here is the conclusion of the matter:*
> *Fear God and keep his commandments,*
> *for this is the whole duty of man.*
> *Ecclesiastes 12:13*

God's Will, Our Initiative

When we make keeping God's law our top priority, it is not a burden, but a delight. The Psalmist shows us what it is to realize God's moral will for what it truly is – good, perfect, and pleasing:

> *Oh, how I love your law!*
>   *I meditate on it all day long.*
> *Your commands make me wiser than my enemies,*
>   *for they are ever with me.*
> *I have more insight than all my teachers,*
>   *for I meditate on your statutes.*
> *I have more understanding than the elders,*
>   *for I obey your precepts.*
> *I have kept my feet from every evil path*
>   *so that I might obey your word.*
> *I have not departed from your laws,*
>   *for you yourself have taught me.*
> *How sweet are your words to my taste,*
>   *sweeter than honey to my mouth!*
> *I gain understanding from your precepts;*
>   *therefore I hate every wrong path.*
>
> *Psalms 119:97-104*

Decision Making

God's sovereign will cannot be thwarted – it is destined to come to pass. God's moral will as revealed in Scripture is the code of conduct reflecting

God's Will

God's character that he desires we live by – and by which he will judge us. Both of these aspects of God's will are taught in the Bible, as we have seen. But, as previously stated there is something different that Christians often mean when they use the term, "God's will". They wonder what choices they should make about what school to attend, what career to pursue, where to live, what ministries to participate in, and a host of other issues. They know that they are bound by God's moral law in these decisions, but that still leaves many options from which to choose. They want to please God by making the best decision. They are asking, "What is God's particular will for me?" and they wonder how to receive guidance from him about these matters. This third meaning of "God's will" may be termed God's individual will for a believer.

Many Christians believe that God has an ideal life-plan for each believer and reveals it to those who have trained themselves to sense God's special guidance in individual matters. However, there is an alternative view maintaining that the Bible does not teach us to try to discern special guidance in choosing between morally-sound opportunities, so we are free to make choices based on wisdom derived from the Bible and other sources. We will examine both sides of the issue in turn.

The Ideal-Plan Approach

The basic premise for the "Ideal-Plan Approach" is that for each of our decisions, God has a perfect plan and it is the believer's responsibility to discover what decisions God wants him or her to make.

For our purposes, the teachings of two prominent Christian leaders of the late nineteenth and early twentieth centuries, George Mueller and F. B. Meyer, will be used as examples of those who support this view. Anyone familiar with contemporary evangelical teaching on the issue of divine guidance will see the influence of these men and their peers.

George Mueller was an English pastor and evangelist most remembered for establishing orphanages and supporting education for underprivileged children. Here is his six-step approach to discerning God's will[2]:

"How to Ascertain the Will of God" by George Mueller

> 1. *I seek at the beginning to get my heart into such a state that it has no will of its own in regard to a given matter. Nine-tenths of the trouble with people generally is just here. Nine-tenths of the difficulties are overcome when our hearts are ready to do the Lord's will whatever it may be. When one is truly in this state, it is usually but a little way to the knowledge of his will.*

---

[2] George Mueller, <u>Answers to Prayer</u> (Moody Press).

2. Having done this, I do not leave the result to feeling or simple impression. If I do so, I make myself liable to great delusions.

3. I seek the will of the Spirit of God through, or in connection with, the Word of God. The Spirit and the Word must be combined. If I look to the Spirit alone without the Word, I lay myself open to great delusions also. If the Holy Ghost guides us at all, He will do it according to the Scriptures and never contrary to them.

4. Next, I take into account providential circumstances. These often plainly indicate God's will in connection with His Word and Spirit.

5. I ask God in prayer to reveal His will to me aright.

6. Thus, through prayer to God, the study of the Word, and reflection, I come to a deliberate judgment according to the best of my ability and knowledge, and if my mind is thus at peace, and continues to be after two or three more petitions, I proceed accordingly. In trivial matters, and in transactions involving most important issues, I have found this method always effective.

Mueller's advice combines lack of passion (step 1: "my heart ... has no will of its own") with Bible study (step 3), providential circumstances (step 4), prayer (step 5), judgment (step 6), and patience (step 6). It is noteworthy that he states that he does not rely on "feeling or simple impression" (step 2), yet is able to "take into account providential circumstances" which "often plainly indicate God's will" (step 4). Most likely, he was saying that he did not make decisions *merely* on the basis of feelings or impressions, but only in combination with the other factors he identified, namely, the Spirit, the Word, and providential circumstances.

F. B. Meyer was an English pastor and evangelist of the generation following Mueller. Some of the teachings of his book, The Secret of Guidance are summarized below[3]:

F. B. Meyer's "Secrets" of Guidance

1. *Our motives must be pure.* "So long as there is some thought of personal advantage, some idea of acquiring the praise and commendation of men, some aim at self aggrandizement, it will be simply impossible to find out God's purpose concerning us."

2. *Our will must be surrendered.* "We must be as plastic clay, ready to take any shape that the great Potter may choose, so shall we be able to detect His guidance."

3. *We must seek information for our mind.* "It is of greatest importance, then, that we should feed our minds with facts, with reliable information, with the

---

[3] F. B. Meyer, The Secret of Guidance (Moody Press). The five principles enumerated here are the titles of section headings of the first chapter. The passage accompanying each principle is excerpted from Meyer's text from the corresponding section.

results of human experience, and (above all) with the teachings of the Word of God."

4. *We must be much in prayer for guidance. "Wrapped in prayer like this, the trustful believer may tread the deck of the ocean steamer night after night, sure that He who points the stars in their courses will not fail to direct the soul that has no other aim than to do His will."*

5. *We must wait the gradual unfolding of God's plan for guidance. "God's impressions within and His Word without are always corroborated by His providence around, and we should quietly wait until these three focus into one point."*

What are the prerequisites for detecting God's guidance, according to Meyer? Pure motives, submission to God, sound information, prayer, and patience. Notice how Meyer's triad of impressions, Scripture and providence coming into focus corresponds so closely with Mueller's remarks about the combination of the Spirit, the Word, and providential circumstances.

Many Christians are greatly comforted in believing that God's individualized guidance is available for each and every decision they must make. Passages such as theses are used to support this belief:

- Proverbs 3:5-6
    *Trust in the LORD with all your heart
    and lean not on your own understanding;*

> in all your ways acknowledge him,
> and he will make your paths straight.

- Psalms 32:8
  > *I will instruct you and teach you in the way you should go; I will counsel you and watch over you.*

- Psalms 23:3
  > *He guides me in paths of righteousness for his name's sake.*

- Isaiah 30:21
  > *Whether you turn to the right or to the left, your ears will hear a voice behind you, saying, "This is the way; walk in it."*

Additionally, Scripture is filled with narrative accounts of God directing individuals in specific actions. Abraham was told by God to leave his country and "go to the land I will show you" (Genesis 12). Moses received God's instructions from a burning bush (Exodus 3). Abraham's servant was directed to select Rebekah to be Isaac's wife (Genesis 24). Gideon was directed by means of a fleece to go to battle against the Midianites (Judges 6).

The Bible is indeed a remarkable record of God's extraordinary work in establishing his kingdom on earth. Many Christians have accepted these examples as representing the norm that God intends for us to follow. They do so even while often experiencing extreme frustration for their inadequacy to detect God's guidance in their own lives.

The Opportunities Approach

The ideal-plan view is so prominent among evangelicals today that many are not even aware that a sound biblical alternative exists. Yet in fact not all believers agree that God has a detailed ideal plan for each individual – or that even if he does, that it can be discerned by means of Scripture, impressions, and providential circumstances.

An alternative framework teaches that the guidance we need to live godly lives is already given us in the Bible, and we should not expect special guidance beyond that. This view stresses the great freedom believers have in making choices and the responsibility we have to decide wisely. First of all, the options we consider must conform to God's moral law. Among those opportunities, we are to make decisions not by trying to detect guidance through impressions or providential circumstances, but rather by applying wisdom gained from Scripture, experience, observations, and counsel.

Garry Friesen, an advocate of this view, provides this summary of a biblical approach to decision making[4]:

---

[4] This summary is presented on Friesen's website, www.gfriesen.net. Further details of Friesen's views may

God's Will, Our Initiative

Friesen's Principles of Decision Making

- *OBEDIENCE*
  – *Where God commands, we must obey.*

- *FREEDOM*
  – *Where there is no command, God gives us freedom (and responsibility) to choose.*

- *WISDOM*
  – *Where there is no command, God gives us wisdom to choose.*

- *HUMBLE TRUST*
  – *When we have chosen what is moral and wise, we must trust the sovereign God to work all the details together for good.*

In place of "impressions" or "providential circumstances" as means for detecting God's guidance, what we see in Friesen's principles is a commitment to grow in maturity so as to make wise decisions concerning the opportunities we face.

The opportunities approach to decision making addresses a problem believers commonly face. Often they want to please God with a decision, but they are

---

be found in <u>Decision Making & the Will of God</u> by Garry Friesen (Multnomah). Also see <u>Finding the Will of God: A Pagan Notion?</u>, by Bruce K. Waltke (Eerdmans), <u>Discovering God's Will</u> by Sinclair B. Ferguson (Banner of Truth), and <u>Just Do Something</u> by Kevin DeYoung (Moody).

not hearing from God what that would be. They try to put their hearts "into such a state that it has no will of its own", to ensure that their motives are pure, and to detect the alignment of Scripture, impressions, and providential circumstances, just as taught by Mueller, Meyer, and contemporary Christian teachers. Once the decision is made, if the results are favorable, this is taken as confirmation that the approach worked. However, if the consequences are adverse, this presents a dilemma: Was the decision wrong because my heart was too corrupt to discern God's leading, or was the decision "right" (that is, consistent with God's leading) and the negative consequences are his means of sanctifying me? Except in cases where the believer has violated God's moral law, the ideal-plan framework offers no means of answering this question. And the question is crucial because one cannot know how to approach future decisions unless it is resolved.

When decisions are approached according to the principles outlined by Friesen, there is no such dilemma. Once we have determined that certain opportunities conform to God's moral will, we are free to select the one we believe to be best. God is pleased that we carefully evaluate each opportunity by the standard of his moral law. God is further pleased if the decision leads to the most effective "good works" that build his kingdom. As we grow in maturity and wisdom, we will tend to make such effective decisions more and more. Adverse consequences enable us to become wiser in making future decisions. The quandary of not knowing how to answer the question of whether or not we followed God's leading does not arise. When we are obeying God's law as taught in Scripture, we *are* following God's leading. In areas where God has given us freedom to decide among opportunities, we exercise that freedom without expecting specific guidance.

How can this view be reconciled with the texts quoted previously, which many Christians regard as referring to finding one's individual ideal life-plan? We have already seen that God is more concerned about decisions involving his moral will than any other decisions we make (1 Corinthians 7:19; Ecclesiastes 12:13; Matthew 6:33). Therefore, why should the passages considered in the previous section (Proverbs 3:5-6, Psalms 32:8, Psalms 23:3, and Isaiah 30:21) be interpreted as promises of guidance in individual matters rather than as guidance in obeying God's moral will? Read them again and you will see that they make perfect sense in the context of obeying God's moral law.

Examples from Scripture where God had an "Individual Will" for those he used to implement his sovereign plan of deliverance for his people are important for us to understand. They provide assurance of God's love for his people and that we can trust him to keep his promises. But shouldn't these be viewed as special cases, rather than the norm to be expected in the lives of all believers? In most Scriptural accounts of individualized guidance, we are told little or nothing about how God communicated to these individuals what he wanted them to do. So how would we know how to follow their examples? An exception is when Gideon sought confirmation from God by means of a fleece before he was willing to carry out what God had instructed him to do. God consented to Gideon's plea, but wouldn't he have been more pleased if Gideon had obeyed him from the beginning?

What a difference it is to see ourselves free to choose from many opportunities. Rather than being prone to anxiety over "missing God's best" by not making the one and only "correct" decision, this approach to decision making leads to gratitude that God has provided multiple opportunities from which to choose. The freedom God gives us to select from among these opportunities requires that we gain wisdom and maturity in order to be effective in his service. This will be addressed in the chapters that follow.

The Master's Will

In the Parable, the servants knew their master wanted them to use the money he entrusted to them to earn a profit. Though we are not told, it is reasonable to assume that he had established boundaries that they were not to violate; for example, that they were to conform to legal and ethical norms. Apparently, within those restrictions, they were free to choose how to put their talents to work.

The servants did not need to rely on special guidance such as "providential circumstances" or "inner impressions" to know what they needed to do. The faithful servants applied wisdom and initiative to accomplish their master's will. And the master was pleased.

Following their example, we will respond to God's will by

- trusting his Sovereign Will,
- obeying his Moral Will, and
- building his kingdom by growing in maturity and applying wisdom.

****

Questions for Discussion and Application

- Many Christians believe that passages such as Proverbs 3:5-6, Psalms 32:8, Psalms 23:3, and Isaiah 30:21 teach that God has an individual life-plan for each person. How do you regard the view that these passages are instead referring to the help God provides to obey his moral will?

God's Will

- Are biblical examples of individualized guidance from God to be expected for all believers, or are they special cases for those having unique roles in God's sovereign plan?

- Do you use different approaches for making major decisions than for minor ones? Why or why not?

****

- Do my thought life and my decisions demonstrate that my primary concerns are to live by God's moral law and to build God's kingdom (Matthew 6:33)?

- In choosing among morally-sound opportunities, would I rather that God tell me the best thing to do or exercise my responsibility to apply wisdom to the best of my ability in making a decision?

- How can I be more diligent in studying God's word so as to understand God's will to be "good, pleasing, and perfect"? (Romans 12:2)

4

Providence

The master provided his servants the resources to fulfill their responsibilities. The clear implication is that each of us is entrusted with resources with which to serve God. This is confirmed repeatedly in Scripture, as in this passage from Paul's letter to the church in Rome:

> *Just as each of us has one body with many members, and these members do not all have the same function, so in Christ we who are many form one body, and each member belongs to all the others. We have different gifts, according to the grace given us.*
> *Romans 12:4-6*

The servants were entrusted with different amounts of money, "each according to his ability" (Matthew 25:15). Likewise, Paul teaches that believers are given different gifts of service "according to the grace given us." The Apostle Peter makes it clear that none is lacking, for God has "given us everything we need" to live so as to please him:

Providence

> *His divine power has given us everything we need for life and godliness through our knowledge of him who called us by his own glory and goodness.*
>
> *2 Peter 1:3*

And so I do not need to ask *if* God has empowered me to serve him. Instead, I should ask, "How can I best put to use the talents God has entrusted to me?" This chapter addresses how the doctrine of God's providence helps to answer that question. Building upon the foundation of the previous two chapters, an understanding of providence will prepare us for learning how to apply wisdom and initiative to best employ our talents in God's service.

The doctrine of God's providence encompasses all aspects of how God superintends over his creation. His constant care is assured:

> *The Son is the radiance of God's glory and the exact representation of his being, sustaining all things by his powerful word...*
>
> *Hebrews 1:3*

> *For by him all things were created: things in heaven and on earth, visible and invisible, whether thrones or powers or rulers or authorities; all things were created by him and for him.*
> *He is before all things, and in him all things hold together.*
>
> *Colossians 1:16-17*

God's Will, Our Initiative

There is widespread understanding among Christians that God lovingly superintends over his creation, but there are differences regarding just how he does so – specifically in regards to the individual responsibility of each believer to determine his or her role in carrying out God's mission of building his kingdom on earth. We will begin by looking at the scriptural basis for making a distinction between "ordinary providence" and "special providence". Next we will see what the life of Paul has to teach us about God's providence, and then return again to the Parable. Finally, we will conclude with some words as to how to apply all this to our lives.

Providence – Ordinary and Special

Most Christians recognize a distinction between ordinary and special providence, but do not necessarily use the terms in the same ways. For our purposes, we will use these definitions[5]:

> <u>Ordinary Providence</u>: *The means God typically uses to govern the world. Created things operating according their created properties. Natural.*
>
> <u>Special Providence</u>: *Any other means by which God interacts with his creation. Supernatural.*

---

[5] See C. John Collins, <u>Science & Faith: Friends or Foes?</u> (Crossway Books), 2008, pp. 163-4.

Providence

Sometimes Christians who are not be familiar with these terms *per se* allude to the distinction between these two aspects of providence without even realizing it. We encountered the phrase "providential circumstances" in Chapter 3 in connection with seeking guidance in making decisions. When believers speak this way, they implicitly refer to special providence. Otherwise the term "providential circumstances" has no real meaning, since everything falls under God's providence in a general sense.

Scripture itself does not use the term "providence", but is replete with examples of both ordinary and special providence. Let us look at a few passages to prepare for examining the role of providence in the life of Paul and in the lives of ordinary believers today.

Ordinary Providence

> *"As long as the earth endures,*
> *seedtime and harvest,*
> *cold and heat,*
> *summer and winter,*
> *day and night*
> *will never cease."*
>
> Genesis 8:22

The regularity of natural processes on a daily, seasonal, or annual basis is evidence of ordinary providence at work. God expects us to be aware of these things. Scripture often uses examples of ordinary providence to teach spiritual truths by analogy, as when Jesus illustrates how to be on guard against false prophets who "come to you in sheep's clothing":

> *By their fruit you will recognize them. Do people pick grapes from thornbushes, or figs from thistles?*
> *Matthew 7:16*

Jesus is saying, "Use your common sense." He fully expects his audience to have a basic grasp of ordinary providence. A tree or plant can always be identified by its fruit. That is the way of nature, as God has ordained it to operate.

Special Providence

> *Then Moses stretched out his hand over the sea, and all that night the LORD drove the sea back with a strong east wind and turned it into dry land. The waters were divided, and the Israelites went through the sea on dry ground, with a wall of water on their right and on their left.*
> *Exodus 14:21-22*

The parting of the sea, allowing the Israelites to escape from captivity in Egypt, is a powerful example of special providence. God may have parted the sea by means of a natural force – namely, the wind – but he caused the wind to behave in an extraordinary way and at just the right time for the Israelites to pass through. Then he restored ordinary providence precisely when needed to foil the Egyptian army's pursuit (Exodus 14:26-28).

Another account of special providence during the life of Moses serves to highlight the distinction between special and ordinary providence. As the Israelites wandered in the desert prior to entering Canaan, a group of 250 men led by Korah rebelled against Moses' leadership. The threat was so serious that it demanded God's special intervention. God directed Moses to make a public spectacle of the insurrectionists' demise as a warning to others not to oppose God's appointed leader:

> *Then Moses said, "This is how you will know that the LORD has sent me to do all these things and that it was not my idea: If these men die a natural death and experience only what usually happens to men, then the LORD has not sent me.*
>
> *"But if the LORD brings about something totally new, and the earth opens its mouth and swallows them, with everything that belongs to them, and they go down alive into the grave, then you will know that these men have treated the LORD with contempt."*
>
> Numbers 16:28-30

The terms "natural" and "what usually happens" in this passage are in essence the very definition of ordinary providence we are using. And when Moses speaks of "something totally new", he is, of course, referring to an act of special providence.

There are at least two things for us to learn from this passage. The most obvious is that our top priority is to honor God under all circumstances. Korah and his followers were guilty of treating the Lord with contempt (v. 30). Secondly, we learn that when it is necessary for us to distinguish an event as special providence, God makes it obvious. There was no room for doubt that Korah and his followers were brought to justice by "providential circumstances" (see Numbers 16:31-33).

Providence in the Life of Paul

The biblical account of Paul's life is filled with acts of special providence, beginning with the immediate events leading to his conversion, as recorded in the Book of Acts. Saul, as he was then known, was on his way to Damascus, intent on arresting any Christians he found there. Suddenly Jesus spoke to him and he was blinded. After three days, a believer named Ananias was directed to meet him. Picking up the account at that point, we read:

> *Then Ananias went to the house and entered it. Placing his hands on Saul, he said, "Brother Saul, the Lord – Jesus, who appeared to you on the*

Providence

road as you were coming here – has sent me so that you may see again and be filled with the Holy Spirit."

Immediately, something like scales fell from Saul's eyes, and he could see again. He got up and was baptized, and after taking some food, he regained his strength.

Acts 9:17-19

This brief passage describes five specific acts of special providence:

- *Ananias went to the house.* Ananias went to the house where Saul had been taken only because God commanded him in a vision to do so (Acts 9:10-12).

- *Jesus, who appeared to you.* Jesus had spoken to Saul three days earlier (Acts 9:4-6).

- *Be filled with the Holy Spirit.* An act of special providence solely of God's doing.

- *He could see again.* Saul's sight was restored after three days of blindness.

- *He got up and was baptized.* Most Christian traditions view baptism as more than simply symbolic, even if there is not complete agreement over the nature of the special providence that baptism entails.

God's Will, Our Initiative

It is interesting that though this three-day period was jam-packed with acts of special providence, this passage concludes with a simple statement of ordinary providence: "... after taking some food, he regained his strength." Apparently, God exercises special providence when required, but only when required. When ordinary providence suffices, that is God's preferred means of accomplishing his purposes.

The Book of Acts documents many works of special providence in the early history of the church. But there is reason to believe that such events were exceptions rather than the rule. Much of what was involved in spreading the gospel was accomplished by believers making wise decisions, applying initiative, and then diligently implementing their plans by means of plain hard work. Consider these passages and what they suggest about Paul's expectations for "providential circumstances" to guide him:

- So when we could stand it no longer, *we thought it best* to be left by ourselves in Athens. (1 Thessalonians 3:1)

- But *I think it is necessary* to send back to you Epaphroditus ... (Philippians 2:25)

- *If it seems advisable* for me to go also, they will accompany me. (1 Corinthians 16:4)

Providence

In each case, Paul gives an account of what had led him to make certain decisions about his plans or the tasks he is assigning to his companions. There is no indication that Paul had received or expected to receive special guidance from God as to what to do. On the contrary, Paul is reaching conclusions through the ordinary process of reasoning. Particularly in the third case, it seems clear that Paul is open to changing his mind – as the situation changes or new information becomes available.

The supernatural work of the Holy Spirit was essential in the work of the early Church – and no one knew that better than Paul. However, it appears that Paul did not expect acts of special providence in every situation. And in the case of his "thorn in the flesh", he sought an act of special providence – that the thorn be taken away – but it was not granted (2 Corinthians 12:7-9). Paul would have to continue to deal with the natural consequences of the thorn.

Paul's writings do not dwell on the hardships he experienced, but neither does he shy away from pointing them out when necessary. The following passage is another example:

> *I have worked much harder, been in prison more frequently, been flogged more severely, and been exposed to death again and again.*

> *Five times I received from the Jews the forty lashes minus one.*
>
> *Three times I was beaten with rods, once I was stoned, three times I was shipwrecked, I spent a night and a day in the open sea, I have been constantly on the move.*
>
> *I have been in danger from rivers, in danger from bandits, in danger from my own countrymen, in danger from Gentiles; in danger in the city, in danger in the country, in danger at sea; and in danger from false brothers.*
>
> *I have labored and toiled and have often gone without sleep; I have known hunger and thirst and have often gone without food; I have been cold and naked.*
>
> 2 Corinthians 11:23-27

Paul was not complaining. His words teach us of the harsh realities of ordinary providence, especially for one fully committed to building God's kingdom. We would do well to follow his example. Although his life was filled with experiences of God's special providence, it appears that typically Paul did not expect God's special guidance or deliverance. He seems to have routinely made decisions based on his own best judgment, while always being prepared to respond to God's intervention.

Providence

Providence in the Parable

Let us again consider the Parable. Does it not teach that God uses ordinary means to build his kingdom? The master went away on a journey and would not be in contact with the servants to guide them or help them. Before he left, he gave each servant an amount of money commensurate with his ability to put it to use and gain a profit. The first servant "went at once and put his money to work," diligently honoring the master's wishes, and the second servant did the same. Their success was simply the natural consequence of their actions, not requiring any acts of special providence. The third servant's failure was the natural consequence of his inaction.

In like manner, Paul uses the sowing of seed and the reaping of a harvest as an analogy for how spiritual growth is achieved in the life of a believer:

> *Do not be deceived: God cannot be mocked. A man reaps what he sows*
>
> *The one who sows to please his sinful nature, from that nature will reap destruction; the one who sows to please the Spirit, from the Spirit will reap eternal life.*
>
> *Let us not become weary in doing good, for at the proper time we will reap a harvest if we do not give up.*
>
> Galatians 6:7-9

The Parable describes how each servant "reaped what he sowed." The third servant was "one who sows to please his sinful nature" – in his case, by being lazy – and he reaped destruction. Each of the first two servants was as "one who sows to please the Spirit." They did not become weary in doing good, and they reaped the harvest of sharing their master's happiness.

Paul's analogy of sowing and reaping reinforces the message of the Parable that diligence and hard work by believers is essential in God's plan for spiritual growth and the spread of the gospel.

Special Providence in Our Lives

God acts supernaturally in all believers to help us obey his moral will and live godly lives. First of all, every believer experiences God's special providence in receiving Christ as Savior. This is not a decision we make on our own, as we have already seen:

> *For it is by grace you have been saved, through faith – and this not from yourselves, it is the gift of God – not by works, so that no one can boast.*
> *Ephesians 2:8-9*

Once we are Christians, God continues to work in our lives to help us obey him. The verse from the Book of 2nd Peter quoted at the beginning of the chapter assures us that God provides what we need to live so as to please him. This he does on an ongoing basis, as we learn from Paul:

> ... for it is God who works in you to will and to act according to his good purpose.
> Philippians 2:13

Ordinary Providence in Our Lives

Just as Paul's own decision making reflects that it was necessary for him to use his judgment and initiative when special providence was not forthcoming, so he teaches other believers to do the same. The verse prior to Philippians 2:13 (quoted above) teaches that we each bear a measure of responsibility for our spiritual growth:

> Therefore, my dear friends, as you have always obeyed – not only in my presence, but now much more in my absence – continue to work out your salvation with fear and trembling ...
> Philippians 2:12

We know that the aspect of salvation Paul is speaking of cannot be that of justification – that is, Jesus' righteousness imputed to us – since that is solely God's doing. When Paul exhorts us to "work out our salvation," he is telling us that growing in godly character – the process of sanctification – is not *solely* God's doing. Our growth also depends upon acts of our wills – choosing to obey God's moral law and to perform good works that build God's kingdom – the very things that earn rewards on the Day of Judgment, as discussed in Chapter 2.

The final results of "working out our salvation" are determined by both God's grace in equipping us and our wisdom and diligence in applying the talents entrusted to us. Our incentive is a prize that lasts for eternity:

> *Do you not know that in a race all the runners run, but only one gets the prize? Run in such a way as to get the prize.*
>
> *Everyone who competes in the games goes into strict training. They do it to get a crown that will not last; but we do it to get a crown that will last forever.*
>
> *Therefore I do not run like a man running aimlessly; I do not fight like a man beating the air. No, I beat my body and make it my slave so that after I have preached to others, I myself will not be disqualified for the prize.*
>
> 1 Corinthians 9:24-27

****

The emphasis of this chapter has been on understanding the important role of ordinary providence in God's plan to build his kingdom, but we must never lose sight of the fact that God does act supernaturally in all believers to help us obey his moral will and live so as to please him. This is not something we could ever earn or deserve – it is solely of his grace. Our proper response is one of gratitude – giving thanks in all circumstances (1 Thessalonians 5:18).

If we are to follow Paul's example and teaching – and the example of the faithful servants of the Parable – we will not expect "providential circumstances" to guide us or to deliver us from the natural consequences of our actions. Of course, should God choose to operate outside of ordinary providence, we will be grateful and adjust our plans and goals accordingly.

Finally, we are to respond to God's providence by recognizing that we reap what we sow. Are you dissatisfied with some aspect of your life? Examine the seed you are sowing. If you are sowing good seed, do not become weary. Continue to sow and care for your crop, and patiently await a good harvest. But an honest evaluation might reveal that your disappointing harvest is the natural result of a failure on your part. Seek the wisdom to realize the change that is necessary, and take the initiative to implement it. These steps are the subjects of the next two chapters.

******

Questions for Discussion and Application

- Is it necessary to know if a particular event is an act of ordinary providence or of special providence? How does this affect decision making?

- Since the Bible does not teach how to distinguish between ordinary and special providence, why do so many Christians believe that God guides believers by means of "providential circumstances"?

- "When ordinary providence suffices, that is God's preferred means of accomplishing his purposes." Do you agree? If so, how do we put this principle into practice?

- C. S. Lewis wrote, "God seems to do nothing Himself that He can possibly delegate to His creatures." How does this relate to an understanding of providence?

****

- Am I satisfied with what I am reaping? (Or, most importantly, is God satisfied?) What am I going to do about it?

- Paul disciplined himself so as not to be disqualified for the prize (1 Corinthians 9:27). In what areas of my life do I need to apply more discipline?

5

Wisdom

With their master away and out of contact with them, the servants could not rely on "providential circumstances" to guide them. Accomplishing their mission required that they be wise in making decisions about how to use the resources entrusted to them.

Everyone wants to be wise. We all have experienced the painful consequences brought about by foolish decisions. So when we read a passage that extols the virtues of wisdom – like this from Proverbs – we assent to it unquestioningly:

> *Wisdom is supreme; therefore get wisdom.*
>   *Though it cost all you have, get understanding.*
> *Esteem her, and she will exalt you;*
>   *embrace her, and she will honor you.*
> *She will set a garland of grace on your head*
>   *and present you with a crown of splendor.*
>   *Proverbs 4:7-9*

When we so glibly affirm this teaching, perhaps we do so without fully considering the imperative of verse 7, "Though it cost all you have, get understanding." We tell ourselves we are willing to do whatever it takes to become wise, but do we stop and ask just how costly wisdom is? A full understanding of what Scripture teaches about acquiring wisdom reveals that the cost is high indeed – in terms of discipline, sacrifice, and hardship.

Warnings Against Wisdom

A good place to begin studying what the Bible teaches about wisdom is to look at its warnings about how prone we are to delude ourselves into thinking we are wise.

> *Do not be wise in your own eyes;*
> *fear the LORD and shun evil.*
> *Proverbs 3:7*

True wisdom, the proverb teaches, begins with honoring God and seeking to obey his moral will. The prophet Jeremiah dismisses the value of anything regarded as wisdom that is contrary to the truths of Scripture:

> *The wise will be put to shame;*
> *they will be dismayed and trapped.*
> *Since they have rejected the word of the LORD,*
> *what kind of wisdom do they have?*
> *Jeremiah 8:9*

Though we be wise in our own eyes – and perhaps esteemed as wise by everyone around us, our wisdom leads to ruin if it is not based on God's standards as revealed in Scripture.

Paul also warns of the inadequacy of mere human wisdom (e.g., 1 Corinthians 1:17, 2:5, 2:13) and declares that "the foolishness of God is wiser than man's wisdom (1 Corinthians 1:25). And James associates "earthly" wisdom with actually denying the truth:

> But if you harbor bitter envy and selfish ambition in your hearts, do not boast about it or deny the truth. Such "wisdom" does not come down from heaven but is earthly, unspiritual, of the devil.
> James 3:14-15

Such wisdom is not the supreme wisdom that the proverb teaches us is worth all cost. The wisdom that the Bible calls us to seek is a wisdom grounded on God's values.

Godly Wisdom

After describing wisdom that is "earthly, unspiritual, and of the devil", James lists some of the traits that accompany godly wisdom, or as he calls it, the "wisdom that comes from heaven."

> But the wisdom that comes from heaven is first of all pure; then peace-loving, considerate, submissive, full of mercy and good fruit, impartial and sincere.
> James 3:17

God's Will, Our Initiative

When Jesus taught that "wisdom is proved right by her actions" (Matthew 11:19), surely the qualities associated with wisdom in this passage are among the things he was referring to. Below we examine more about what Scripture has to say about each of these attributes of godly wisdom.

Pure

The first quality in James' description of wisdom is purity.

> *Listen, my son, and be wise,*
>   *and keep your heart on the right path.*
>   *Proverbs 23:19*

The wise son is one whose heart is "on the right path," that is, on the path of obedience to God's moral law. We saw in Chapter 3 that the principal aim of God's will for our lives is that we honor him by obeying his moral law. So the mark of a wise person is a life of obedience.

> *Who is wise? He will realize these things. Who is discerning? He will understand them. The ways of the LORD are right; the righteous walk in them, but the rebellious stumble in them.*
>   *Hosea 14:9*

Wisdom

Peace-loving

Next James identifies wisdom as peace-loving, in contrast to the envy and selfish ambition of earthly wisdom. Proverbs teaches us that those who are wise have learned to diffuse others' anger and thereby promote peace:

> *Mockers stir up a city,*
>   *but wise men turn away anger.*
> *If a wise man goes to court with a fool,*
>   *the fool rages and scoffs, and there is no peace.*
>   Proverbs 29:8-9

Even the most powerful of men – a king with the authority to impose a death sentence and have it executed immediately – can be calmed by one trained in wisdom:

> *A king's wrath is a messenger of death,*
>   *but a wise man will appease it.*
>   Proverbs 16:14

The wise are "slow to become angry" (James 1:19) and are a peaceful influence to those around them.

Gentleness

The third quality that James associates with wisdom is translated "considerate" in the New International Version, but is more commonly translated "gentle". Peter teaches that believers should be gentle and respectful when presenting a reasoned argument for their faith:

> *But in your hearts set apart Christ as Lord. Always be prepared to give an answer to everyone who asks you to give the reason for the hope that you have. But do this with gentleness and respect...*
> *1 Peter 3:15*

Reverence

Next, James identifies submissiveness as a characteristic of godly wisdom. We will look at three aspects of submissiveness – first, a reverence for God; then, humility; and finally, a teachable spirit. Reverence for God is often referred to in Scripture as "the fear of the Lord":

> *The fear of the LORD is the beginning of wisdom,*
> *and knowledge of the Holy One is understanding.*
> *Proverbs 9:10*

> *He will be the sure foundation for your times,*
>   *a rich store of salvation and wisdom and knowledge;*
> *the fear of the LORD is the key to this treasure.*
> *Isaiah 33:6*

The lack of reverence for God is why mere human reason is futile, but the fear of the Lord, Isaiah tells us, unlocks the storehouse of wisdom that God intends for his children.

Wisdom

Humility

Another aspect of godly submission is the quality of humility. Note that taken together, the following two passages teach that humility is both a prerequisite for wisdom and a result of wisdom:

> *When pride comes, then comes disgrace,*
> *but with humility comes wisdom.*
> Proverbs 11:2

> *Who is wise and understanding among you? Let him show it by his good life, by deeds done in the humility that comes from wisdom.*
> James 3:13

That Scripture describes humility as both a prerequisite and result of wisdom is not contradictory. The same is true of all the qualities associated with wisdom. As we develop godly character, we enhance our ability to grow in wisdom, and this in turn further develops that character.

Being Teachable

A third aspect of godly submission is having a teachable spirit. Consider what these proverbs say about how those who are wise listen to advice:

> *Listen to advice and accept instruction,*
> *and in the end you will be wise.*
> Proverbs 19:20

> *Instruct a wise man and he will be wiser still;*
> *teach a righteous man and he will add to his*
> *learning.*
> Proverbs 9:9

> *He who listens to a life-giving rebuke*
> *will be at home among the wise.*
> Proverbs 15:31

Those who are wise recognize that they still have much to learn. They value the advice of others so much that they are willing to receive instruction even in the form of rebuke.

Full of Mercy and Good Fruit

The qualities that accompany wisdom produce the same good fruit that result from resisting the sinful nature and living according to the Holy Spirit:

> *But the fruit of the Spirit is love, joy, peace, patience, kindness, goodness, faithfulness, gentleness and self-control.*
> Galatians 5:22-23

The "good fruit" James speaks of is expressed both in godly character and in the "good deeds" that God uses to build his kingdom (James 3:13). Godly wisdom is not passive. It transforms who we are and affects everything we do.

Wisdom

Impartiality

Earlier in his letter, James warns against showing favoritism based on superficial appearances (James 2:1-13), and now he lists impartiality as an attribute of godly wisdom. Judging wisely also entails basing one's judgment of others on their actions rather than supposing that we can discern the true intentions of anyone's heart but our own. As Jesus taught in the Sermon on the Mount:

> *Do not judge, or you too will be judged. For in the same way you judge others, you will be judged, and with the measure you use, it will be measured to you.*
> *Matthew 7:1-2*

Later in his sermon, Jesus instructs us to beware of false prophets, and that "by their fruit you will recognize them" (Matthew 7:15). So we know that Jesus was warning not about judging another's actions, but rather judging another's motives. A wise person judges his own heart, but understands that he cannot fully know another's motives or intentions (1 Corinthians 2:11).

Sincerity

The final quality James lists is that of sincerity. In writing to the Corinthians, Paul speaks of the sincerity with which he ministered to them and attributes it to a wisdom not of the world, but from God:

> *Now this is our boast: Our conscience testifies that we have conducted ourselves in the world, and especially in our relations with you, in the holiness and sincerity that are from God. We have done so not according to worldly wisdom but according to God's grace.*
> 2 Corinthians 1:12

All the qualities James associates with wisdom – purity, peace, gentleness, submissiveness, mercy, good fruit, impartiality, and sincerity – are both prerequisites for wisdom and the results of applying wisdom. Do you want to grow in wisdom? Everyone says they do. However, the cost is high in terms of the discipline required to develop godly character. How much do you want the qualities Scripture associates with wisdom to characterize your life? Are you really willing to pay the price?

Sources of Wisdom

Wisdom is a matter of both heart and mind. We have already seen that committing ourselves to developing godly character is the first step in growing in wisdom, and now we consider what to feed our minds. In Chapter 3, we encountered F. B. Meyer's answer, and it is worth repeating:

Wisdom

> "It is of greatest importance, then, that we should feed our minds with facts, with reliable information, with the results of human experience, and (above all) with the teachings of the Word of God."

Meyer calls us to search broadly for knowledge while maintaining Scripture as the ultimate authority. Centuries earlier, the great English scholar Francis Bacon put it like this:

> "... let no man ... think ... that a man can search too far, or be too well studied in the Book of God's Word, or in the Book of God's Works..."

Theologians often make this distinction by referring to Scripture (Book of God's Word) as "special revelation" and other sources of knowledge (Book of God's Works) as "general revelation". Using this distinction, we will now examine what Scripture says about itself as a source of knowledge and wisdom and then what it says about sources outside of itself.

Special Revelation

> *Your word is a lamp to my feet*
> *and a light for my path.*
>
> Ps 119:105

Scripture is essential as a source of wisdom in directing us how to live. Paul describes Scripture as the very breath of God, given to us so that we will grow in righteousness and be equipped for building God's kingdom by our good works:

> *All Scripture is God-breathed and is useful for teaching, rebuking, correcting and training in righteousness, so that the man of God may be thoroughly equipped for every good work.*
> *2 Timothy 3:16-17*

Scripture challenges us and exposes our weaknesses.

> *For the word of God is living and active. Sharper than any double-edged sword, it penetrates even to dividing soul and spirit, joints and marrow; it judges the thoughts and attitudes of the heart.*
> *Hebrews 4:12*

No other book is "living and active" like God's word. To grow in wisdom, we must learn to "correctly handle the word of truth" (2 Timothy 2:15) and "meditate on it day and night, so that you may be careful to do everything written in it" (Joshua 1:8).

<u>General Revelation</u>

We have seen that Scripture warns against ungodly wisdom – wisdom based on human reasoning alone – but extols wisdom that is grounded in godly values. And while Scripture declares itself to be superior as a source of knowledge on which to

Wisdom

base our lives, it in no way excludes other sources as legitimate means for believers to use in making decisions. We will consider three categories of such "general revelation" and see what the Bible says about applying them in daily life: 1) personal observations and research, 2) experience, and 3) counsel.

• Personal Observations and Research

Jesus challenged his disciples to "count the cost" of following him with these words:

> *Suppose one of you wants to build a tower. Will he not first sit down and estimate the cost to see if he has enough money to complete it? For if he lays the foundation and is not able to finish it, everyone who sees it will ridicule him, saying, "This fellow began to build and was not able to finish."*
>
> *Or suppose a king is about to go to war against another king. Will he not first sit down and consider whether he is able with ten thousand men to oppose the one coming against him with twenty thousand? If he is not able, he will send a delegation while the other is still a long way off and will ask for terms of peace.*
>
> Luke 14:28-32

Jesus presents two scenarios involving important decisions to be made. The wisdom of "sitting down" and carefully evaluating a situation before deciding what to do is so obvious that he expresses it by means of a rhetorical question. Jesus is taking for granted the value of personal observations and research as necessary components of making wise decisions.

- Experience

The second aspect of general revelation we need to employ to grow in wisdom is experience. God does not expect us to accept the teaching of Scripture apart from personal experience, but rather instructs us to "taste and see" for ourselves.

> *Taste and see that the LORD is good:*
> *blessed is the man who takes refuge in him.*
> *Psalm 34:8*

Solomon was a man known far and wide for his great wisdom (1 Kings 4:34). In the book of Ecclesiastes, he writes from the vantage point of an old man who has learned from years of observation and experience (Ecclesiastes 1:16):

> *I thought to myself, "Look, I have grown and increased in wisdom more than anyone who has ruled over Jerusalem before me; I have experienced much of wisdom and knowledge."*

And when Scripture declares that gray hair is "the splendor of the old" (Proverbs 20:29), it is the wisdom of experience that makes it so.

- Counsel

Along with observations, research, and experience, the counsel of reliable advisors is a necessary component of wise decision making. We have already discussed that to be wise requires that we be teachable, so it might seem redundant to return to this point. However, it is of such importance that we consult with people who can provide a fresh perspective based on their own observation, their experiences, and the counsel they have received from yet others that it bears repeating.

> *Plans fail for lack of counsel,*
> *but with many advisers they succeed.*
> *Proverbs 15:22*

> *For lack of guidance a nation falls,*
> *but many advisers make victory sure.*
> *Proverbs 11:14*

> *The way of a fool seems right to him,*
> *but a wise man listens to advice.*
> *Proverbs 12:15*

Gaining Wisdom

Growing in wisdom, as has already been said, is a matter of both heart and mind. It begins with a commitment to develop godly character – purity, peace, gentleness, submissiveness, mercy, impartiality, sincerity, and all the fruit of the Spirit.

It is fed by active study of both God's word (special revelation) and God's works (general revelation). And the final element of gaining wisdom is perseverance, for wisdom is not attained easily. James describes the necessity of perseverance for wisdom as follows:

> *Consider it pure joy, my brothers, whenever you face trials of many kinds, because you know that the testing of your faith develops perseverance.*
>
> *Perseverance must finish its work so that you may be mature and complete, not lacking anything.*
>
> *If any of you lacks wisdom, he should ask God, who gives generously to all without finding fault, and it will be given to him.*
> *James 1:2-5*

Trials and testing develop perseverance, James tells us. And perseverance is required to be mature and complete – which is to say, to be wise. And the promise that God gives wisdom to those who ask (v. 5) – is this some kind of shortcut that avoids the pain of trials and testing? No. Instead, God grants wisdom by allowing us to experience the very hardships and difficulties that develop perseverance.

This is why we are told that wisdom is so costly (Proverbs 4:7). It costs us everything. We gain wisdom only as our whole character is transformed and as we diligently apply the resources entrusted to us to build God's kingdom.

Wisdom

****

Therefore everyone who hears these words of mine and puts them into practice is like a wise man who built his house on the rock. The rain came down, the streams rose, and the winds blew and beat against that house; yet it did not fall, because it had its foundation on the rock.
Matthew 7:24-25

****

Questions for Discussion and Application

- For many Christians, it seems that the goal of wisdom is to detect individualized guidance by interpreting providential circumstances. How does this compare with what the Bible teaches about wisdom?

- Can godly wisdom be developed without the trials and hardships described in James 1:2-5?

****

- Of the qualities that accompany wisdom, which are the ones that I most need to develop?

- Am I studying the Bible enough to grow in wisdom?

- What must I do the become a better student both of God's word (special revelation) and of God's works (general revelation)?

God's Will, Our Initiative

- Who are my counselors?

- Do I learn from failures and hardships? Am I easily frustrated by them or do I persevere with joy because I recognize their value in developing wisdom and maturity?

6

Initiative

The servants were not given specific plans from their master, so it was necessary that they exercise initiative. The master did not tell them how to utilize their talents. It was each servant's responsibility to apply wisdom in creating and choosing opportunities and then to implement his decisions. And so we must ask: *Do I have the freedom (and responsibility) to choose how I serve God?*

Some will object to regarding human initiative in a favorable light. After all, the initiative undertaken by Adam and Eve to disobey God condemned the entire human race to alienation from God. And speaking for all humanity, Paul described his sinful nature as being a "slave to the law of sin" (Romans 7:25). When we are set free from our sinful nature by coming to Christ, it is not by our own initiative, but by God's initiative to grant us faith (Ephesians 2:8-9). The good deeds we perform in service to God are a response to God's grace – the motivation does not originate in us.

However, as we have seen in previous chapters, the extent to which God chooses to build his kingdom by means of ordinary providence (and not solely special providence) necessitates that believers use their own powers of reasoning – consistent with Scripture and general revelation – to grow in wisdom and make the most of available opportunities. I don't know of a better term than "initiative" to describe the activity of exercising our freedom to choose among opportunities of service, as long as we remember that it is only by God's grace that we choose to serve him in the first place and that we have the talents to do so.

In using the term "initiative" to describe how God wants us to serve him, I mean "godly initiative", defined as follows:

> **Godly Initiative:** In humble submission to God's authority, acting with the intention of using one's resources as effectively as possible to build God's kingdom.

It is in this sense that Paul used the term in writing to commend his co-worker Titus:

> I thank God, who put into the heart of Titus the same concern I have for you. For Titus not only welcomed our appeal, but he is coming to you with much enthusiasm and on his own initiative.
> 2 Corinthians 8:16-17

Paul and his associates were constantly evaluating the needs of the churches and making decisions about how to best employ their resources to help them. In this case, Titus determined that his best opportunity of service was to visit the Christians in Corinth. Paul agreed that this was a wise choice, and Titus' enthusiasm helped convince Paul that this was the best decision.

We will see that this is but one example in Scripture of godly initiative, that is, believers making and implementing godly decisions without a specific directive from God. After surveying several other examples, we will consider biblical appeals to exercise initiative and the role of diligence in seeing our work through to completion.

Biblical Examples of Godly Initiative

Acts of special providence fill the pages of Scripture, of course, but as has already been argued, this in no way excludes ordinary providence as the primary means God uses to build his kingdom. In this section, we will look at examples from both the Old and New Testaments. From the Old Testament, we will consider Jethro, Esther, and Isaiah. From the New Testament, we will look at Luke, the elders in the Jerusalem church, and Paul and his coworkers.

Jethro: "What you are doing is not good ..."

Soon after Moses led the Israelites out of Egypt, his father-in-law Jethro joined them and observed

Moses wearing himself out by single-handedly adjudicating disputes among the people "from morning till evening" (Exodus 18:14). Jethro confronted Moses with a strong dose of common sense:

> Moses' father-in-law replied, "What you are doing is not good. You and these people who come to you will only wear yourselves out. The work is too heavy for you; you cannot handle it alone. Listen now to me and I will give you some advice, and may God be with you."
> Exodus 18:17-19

Jethro then proposes that Moses delegate responsibility to trustworthy men, appointing them as officials "over thousands, hundreds, fifties and tens" for the simple cases, reserving only the difficult cases for Moses to decide. This solution seems like it should have been obvious to Moses, but in the midst of the stress of all his responsibilities, apparently it hadn't occurred to him. Fortunately, Moses had the wisdom to take Jethro's advice and "did everything he said" (Exodus 18:24).

There is no indication that Jethro received special insight from God. He simply took the initiative to propose a plan reasoned from general revelation.

Esther: "Who knows ...?"

The Book of Esther is the account of how a plan to exterminate the Jews of Persia was thwarted by a

Initiative

young Jewish woman whose beauty so enthralled King Xerxes he had made her his wife. When Esther's cousin Mordecai uncovered the plot of the evil prime minister Haman, he implored Esther to approach the king and stop Haman from implementing his plan. Fearing for her life – as approaching the king uninvited was punishable by death – Esther balked at Mordecai's plea that she intervene on behalf of her people. Read how Mordecai pressed the case for Esther to take the risk:

> When Esther's words were reported to Mordecai, he sent back this answer:
>
> "Do not think that because you are in the king's house you alone of all the Jews will escape. For if you remain silent at this time, relief and deliverance for the Jews will arise from another place, but you and your father's family will perish. And who knows but that you have come to royal position for such a time as this?"
>
> Esther 4:12-14

Mordecai's response is interesting. He does not promise that God will protect Esther or that her actions would save the Jews. He admits that he does not know what will happen, except he is sure that one way or another, God will not allow the Jews to be destroyed. He does not minimize the risk he is asking Esther to take, but appeals to her on the basis of doing what is right. Esther is in a position that provides her an opportunity to attempt to intervene, and Mordecai reasons that she is obligated to try.

Esther is persuaded that she must take initiative: "I will go to the king, even though it is against the law. And if I perish, I perish." (Esther 4:16). She takes great care in choosing how to express her request and succeeds in having the king reverse the royal edict, thereby saving the Jews.

Isaiah: "Send me!"

We don't tend to think of the prophets of the Old Testament as volunteering for their office, but that is the way Isaiah describes his experience:

> *Then I heard the voice of the Lord saying, "Whom shall I send? And who shall go for us? And I said, "Here am I. Send me!"*
>
> *Isaiah 6:8*

Luke: "It seemed good ..."

The inspiration of Scripture is an act of special providence, to be sure. So, in explaining why he wrote the gospel account that bears his name, one might have expected Luke to say, "God told me to do it." But Luke put it very differently:

> *Therefore, since I myself have carefully investigated everything from the beginning, it seemed good also to me to write an orderly*

Initiative

> account for you, most excellent Theophilus, so that you may know the certainty of the things you have been taught.
> *Luke 1:3*

"It seemed good." Again, the language of initiative. Luke wrote because he had the opportunity and it seemed to him that it was the most effective thing he could do to build the kingdom.

Apostles: "It would not be right ..."

In its early days, the church in Jerusalem grew quickly – so much so that the twelve apostles were overwhelmed with their duties. In much the same manner as Jethro had reasoned that Moses needed to delegate responsibility to others so as to allow him to focus on the difficult judicial cases, the apostles reasoned that they needed to assign to others the responsibility for waiting on tables:

> So the Twelve gathered all the disciples together and said, "It would not be right for us to neglect the ministry of the word of God in order to wait on tables.
> Brothers, choose seven men from among you who are known to be full of the Spirit and wisdom. We will turn this responsibility over to them and will give our attention to prayer and the ministry of the word."
> *Acts 6:2-4*

Hence the office of deacon was instituted not by divine decree, but by wisdom applied by men seeking to serve God as effectively as possible – that is, by exercising godly initiative.

Jerusalem Church: "It seemed good ..."

Later, the leaders of the Jerusalem church were faced with the decision of what requirements should be set for the many Gentiles in surrounding regions that were being converted – in particular, whether Jewish practices such as circumcision were necessary. Some, such as James, said no: "It is my judgment, therefore, that we should not make it difficult for the Gentiles who are turning to God." (Acts 15:19). This reasoning carried the day, as evidenced by this excerpt of the letter that was sent to the Gentile believers:

> *It seemed good to the Holy Spirit and to us not to burden you with anything beyond the following requirements:*
> *You are to abstain from food sacrificed to idols, from blood, from the meat of strangled animals and from sexual immorality. You will do well to avoid these things. Farewell.*
> *Acts 15:28-29*

Another important decision of the early church made without the need for special providence, but rather enacted through the initiative taken by its leaders.

Initiative

Paul: "We thought ...", I think ...", "it seems ..."

At many points during his missionary journeys, God directed Paul in unmistakable ways. However, this was not always so. In Chapter 4, we looked at three passages where Paul explained his decisions in ways that indicate that he was not aware of any special providence directing him. In each case, he uses the language of initiative to tell why certain decisions were made.

Paul told the church in Thessalonica that: "We thought it best" to send Timothy to visit them:

> *So when we could stand it no longer, we thought it best to be left by ourselves in Athens. We sent Timothy, who is our brother and God's fellow worker in spreading the gospel of Christ, to strengthen and encourage you in your faith ...*
> *1 Thessalonians 3:1-2*

To the church in Philippi, he wrote that he "thought it necessary" to send Epaphroditus to them:

> *But I think it is necessary to send back to you Epaphroditus, my brother, fellow worker and fellow soldier, who is also your messenger, whom you sent to take care of my needs.*
> *For he longs for all of you and is distressed because you heard he was ill.*
> *Philippians 2:25-26*

And he told the church in Corinth that he was thus far undecided as to whether he would lead a delegation from that congregation to visit Jerusalem, but that he would do so "if it seems advisable..."

> Then, when I arrive, I will give letters of introduction to the men you approve and send them with your gift to Jerusalem. If it seems advisable for me to go also, they will accompany me.
> 1 Corinthians 16:3-4

Particularly in this case, it is clear that Paul was not expecting God to specifically direct his decision, but rather he would continue to evaluate the opportunity to the best of his ability, then take action when he deemed appropriate.

Biblical Appeals for Godly Initiative

The language of initiative is used throughout Scripture to rouse believers into action. It begins in the Garden of Eden, when God told Adam that with one exception – the tree of the knowledge of good and evil – he was "free to eat from any tree in the garden" (Genesis 2:16). Next we are told that God gave Adam the freedom to choose names for "all the livestock, the birds of the air and all the beasts of the field" (Genesis 2:20). Clearly, God created Adam to exercise initiative.

Initiative

Adam and Eve abused that freedom by eating of the forbidden tree (Genesis 3), but that sin did not negate God's intention that his people exercise initiative – godly initiative – in their daily lives. Speaking for all believers, Paul rejoiced "because through Christ Jesus the law of the Spirit of life set me free from the law of sin and death" (Romans 8:2). In other words, we are free to make choices that honor God.

Paul emphasized our freedom when he addressed the issue of remarriage for a Christian woman whose husband has died:

> *A woman is bound to her husband as long as he lives. But if her husband dies, she is free to marry anyone she wishes, but he must belong to the Lord. In my judgment, she is happier if she stays as she is – and I think that I too have the Spirit of God.*
> 1 Corinthians 7:39-40

As Adam and Eve were free to eat from any tree – except for one in particular – so the believing widow is free to marry "anyone she wishes" as long as he is a fellow believer. Paul goes on to express his opinion that she would be wise to remain single, but he does so while making it clear that he respects her right to make her own decision.

Later in the same letter, Paul writes more generally about the freedom we have to make decisions – again, so long as they are consistent with

God's Will, Our Initiative

God's moral will – and he encourages believers to make the choices they believe will honor God the most:

> *So whether you eat or drink or whatever you do, do it all for the glory of God.*
> *1 Corinthians 10:31*

Instead of trying to discern the one-and-only "ideal" choice that God intends, we have the freedom to choose among all morally-sound opportunities. We make our decision by applying the wisdom we have gained through life:

> *Be very careful, then, how you live – not as unwise but as wise, making the most of every opportunity, because the days are evil.*
> *Ephesians 5:15-16*

Time and again, Scripture implores the believer to take the initiative in growing in godliness and serving others:

- Consider how we may spur one another on ...

  > *And let us consider how we may spur one another on toward love and good deeds*
  > *Hebrews 10:24*

- Make every effort ...

  > *For this very reason, make every effort to add to your faith goodness; and to goodness, knowledge and to knowledge, self-control; and to self-control,*

Initiative

> *perseverance; and to perseverance, godliness; and to godliness, brotherly kindness; and to brotherly kindness, love. For if you possess these qualities in increasing measure, they will keep you from being ineffective and unproductive in your knowledge of our Lord Jesus Christ.*
>
> 2 Peter 1:5-8

- As far as it depends on you ...

  > *If it is possible, as far as it depends on you, live at peace with everyone.*
  >
  > Romans 12:18

- Do not become weary ...

  > *Let us not become weary in doing good, for at the proper time we will reap a harvest if we do not give up.*
  >
  > Galatians 6:9

Initiative and Diligence

As wisdom is wasted if it is not accompanied by the initiative to implement a decision, so initiative is of little value if one is not diligent to see a worthy task through to completion. The one who lacks diligence is like the seed in Jesus' parable sown on rocky places, which springs up quickly but withers because the soil is shallow. In contrast, the seed sown on good soil that can support deep roots is highly productive (Matthew 13).

God's Will, Our Initiative

Paul exemplified the diligence that leads to a productive life. We read in Chapter 4 of the extreme hardships he endured for the sake of the gospel (e.g., 2 Corinthians 11:23-27). He did so because he was determined to "finish the race":

> *However, I consider my life worth nothing to me, if only I may finish the race and complete the task the Lord Jesus has given me – the task of testifying to the gospel of God's grace.*
> *Acts 20:24*

Using the same analogy, he encourages all believers to "run in such a way as to get the prize":

> *Do you not know that in a race all the runners run, but only one gets the prize? Run in such a way as to get the prize.*
> *1 Corinthians 9:24*

The prize he refers to is that of hearing the words the master spoke to his faithful servants: "Well done.... Come and share your master's happiness!"

Running the race to win the prize begins with understanding that our destiny includes being held accountable for our lives. It requires a commitment to obey God's moral law and do good works with the talents God has entrusted to us. This we do by gaining wisdom and exercising initiative and diligence to build God's kingdom.

****

Initiative

> **ASK** *(and keep on asking)*
> *and it will be given to you;*
>
> **SEEK** *(and keep on seeking)*
> *and you will find;*
>
> **KNOCK** *(and keep on knocking)*
> *and the door will be opened to you.*
>
> Matthew 7:7
>
> (emphasis and parenthetical comments added)

****

Questions for Discussion and Application

- How would you describe the role of the believer's initiative in building God's kingdom?

- How can we know when to exercise initiative and when to "wait upon the Lord" for him to guide?

- Since God gives us freedom to choose among morally-sound opportunities, is it reasonable to expect him to give us special guidance in making decisions?

****

- Am I failing to contribute to building God's kingdom as best I can ...

God's Will, Our Initiative

- because I am waiting for clearer instructions from God?
- because I'm afraid of failing?
- because someone else is better gifted?
- because I'm lazy?

- What could I do to more effectively build God's kingdom?

7

Mission

We have seen how the Parable is encouraging to believers who faithfully seek to obey God's moral will and do good works that build God's kingdom. Like the faithful servants in the Parable, they look forward to the Master's return, knowing that they will be rewarded. However, there is a dark side to the Parable. The servant who made no attempt to apply his talent was punished and not given another chance. And so we must ask: *Could this happen to me?*

The Parable is not the only time that Jesus warns about living unproductively. On his way to Gethsemane, he told his disciples:

> "I am the true vine, and my Father is the gardener. He cuts off every branch in me that bears no fruit, while every branch that does bear fruit he prunes so that it will be even more fruitful.... If anyone does not remain in me, he is like a branch that is thrown away and withers; such branches are picked up, thrown into the fire and burned."
> *John 15:1-2, 6*

Just as the unproductive servant was thrown outside "into the darkness, where there will be weeping and gnashing of teeth" (Matthew 25:30), here Jesus says that the branch that is unproductive ("bears no fruit") will be cut off from the vine and burned.

From the Book of Hebrews, we receive a similar warning:

> *Land that drinks in the rain often falling on it and that produces a crop useful to those for whom it is farmed receives the blessing of God. But land that produces thorns and thistles is worthless and is in danger of being cursed. In the end it will be burned.*
> *Hebrews 6:7-8*

The third servant was so irresponsible that he did not even invest the money entrusted to him with bankers (Matthew 25:27), but merely hid it. We smugly chastise him and assert that we would never be that foolish. But have you ever failed to use the resources God has entrusted to you to build his kingdom? If so, how can you say that you have not acted just as foolishly as the unfaithful servant who buried his talent? If you consistently fail to employ God's investment in you, will you not become the unfruitful branch that Jesus warns of?

Yet the purpose of Jesus' warning is not to discourage us, but rather to draw us to himself and to spur us on to good deeds.

Mission

> *This is to my Father's glory, that you bear much fruit, showing yourselves to be my disciples.*
> *John 15:8*

Similarly, the passage in Hebrews is a prelude to a message of encouragement and hope:

> *Even though we speak like this, dear friends, we are confident of better things in your case – things that accompany salvation. God is not unjust; he will not forget your work and the love you have shown him as you have helped his people and continue to help them. We want each of you to show this same diligence to the very end, in order to make your hope sure.*
> *Hebrews 6:9-11*

Making our hope sure requires diligence – not giving up, not growing weary in doing good. This is what was lacking in the third servant. The problem was not that he failed while trying to put his talent to use, but that he didn't even try. To the master, this was unacceptable.

One cannot help but wonder what might have happened if he had diligently set out to put his talent to work – as did the first two servants – but due to his inexperience or other circumstances, he failed to gain a return and even lost the original investment the master had entrusted to him. How would the master have responded? We cannot be entirely sure, but certainly the consequences of his failure could not have been worse than the consequences of his inaction.

Scripture teaches that failure can be overcome. Consider these examples from biblical history:

- Jacob deceived his father Isaac and was forced to flee from his brother Esau for fear of his life (Genesis 27).

- Joseph's youthful arrogance so offended his brothers that they sold him into slavery (Genesis 37).

- Moses was forced to flee Pharaoh's court and live in exile as a shepherd after losing his temper and killing an Egyptian (Exodus 2:11-22).

- Elijah was so discouraged that he prayed that God would take away his life (1 Kings 19:1-4).

- Peter denied Christ three times (Matthew 26:69-75).

- John Mark abandoned Paul and Barnabus during their first missionary journey (Acts 13:13), and Paul refused to allow him to rejoin them (Acts 15:36-38).

None of these situations ended with failure. Each served as an opportunity to grow in wisdom and character and to develop perseverance.

Mission

God has assigned every believer the mission of contributing to building his kingdom. He has equipped us with the resources we need to do so. Within the bounds of his moral law, we are free to choose how to employ those resources. We will be held accountable for obeying God's law and performing good deeds that build God's kingdom. We will be rewarded according to our effectiveness. Failures along the way can be overcome if we learn from them and use them to grow in wisdom and godly character. The ultimate failure is to not try.

****

Aware that God will hold me accountable for every detail of my life:

I will live in gratitude for his mercy;

I will obey his moral law;

I will grow in wisdom; and

I will build his kingdom by exercising initiative and diligence in applying the resources entrusted to me.

****

Questions for Discussion and Application

- How does Paul's concern about being "disqualified for the prize" (1 Co 9:27) relate to the warnings of John 15 and Hebrews 6?

God's Will, Our Initiative

- Who are other examples from Scripture of men and women who experienced failure but overcame it for God's glory? Who are some examples from history and the present?

****

- Am I concerned about Scripture's warnings of living an unproductive life?

- Have I buried my talent?

- How can I live more productively for Christ?

EPILOGUE

God's Presence

The Master of the Parable is a loving master. We know this because he entrusted his servants with money and responsibility, he provided them opportunities for meaningful activity, and he generously rewarded their faithfulness. We are quick to recognize these aspects of the Parable as illustrating how our loving heavenly Father cares for us.

But what are we to make of the fact that the Master left the servants completely on their own for "a long time" (Matthew 25:19)? His absence was long enough for the two faithful servants to double their investment, so it is not hard to imagine this being a period of time measured in years. What are we to make of such a remote and distant Master? Does this facet of the story have something to tell us about our relationship with God? Or should we ignore it and focus instead on those qualities of the Master that we are comfortable with?

The thought of God being distant is distressing, and it is contrary to what Scripture teaches. The same Jesus who told the Parable had much to say to his disciples about the close relationship that God seeks to have with his children. He taught us to address God as "Our Father" (Matthew 6:9). He said not to worry about food or clothes, for just as the Father cares for lesser creatures, he provides for our needs (Matthew 6:25-34). The Father knows us intimately, down to the number of hairs on our heads (Matthew 10:30).

Jesus called his disciples his friends (John 15:14), telling them, "As the Father has loved me, so have I loved you" (John 15:9). He likened his relationship with believers to that of branches growing on a vine, using this metaphor to assure us, "Remain in me and I will remain in you" (John 15:4-5). Jesus' final words recorded by Matthew contain the promise, "And surely I am with you always, to the very end of the age" (Matthew 28:20). And if this weren't enough, we have the record of the Apostle John's vision, in which Jesus says, "Here I am! I stand at the door and knock. If anyone hears my voice and opens the door, I will come in and eat with him, and he with me" (Revelation 3:20).

In this context, the Master's long absence is a striking feature of the Parable, seemingly at odds with Jesus' other teachings. So our first inclination might be to dismiss this point. After all, no analogy is perfect. The lessons we can learn from the five major themes of the Parable addressed in this book are so profound, we hardly need be concerned if this particular detail seems inapplicable.

Yet what believer has not experienced times of loneliness when it seems as if God is remote and distant? We long for God's presence, but don't feel it. There is a sense of dryness in our spiritual life. We understand Jeremiah's lament, "Even when I call out or cry for help, he shuts out my prayer" (Lamentations 3:8). Like the Psalmist, we ask,

My God, my God, why have you forsaken me?
 Why are you so far from saving me,
 so far from the words of my groaning?
 O my God, I cry out by day, but you do not answer,
 by night, and am not silent.
                                            Psalm 22:1-2

What is the believer to do during such times? There is no single answer, but perhaps the Parable has something to teach us about what to do when we feel distant from God. The Master was far away and out of contact with his servants, but they knew what they needed to do. Their work was challenging and meaningful, worth every measure of intellect, diligence, and commitment they could muster. The Master had prepared them. He was counting on them. He would return to reward them and give them greater responsibility.

Likewise even when we do not feel God's presence, we know what he wants us to do, for he has revealed it to us in his word. We know what pleases him – growing in godly character, obeying his moral will, and doing good works that build his kingdom. And we know that he will reward us if we are faithful. And – unlike the servants – we are assured that God really is with us at all times, even when we might not feel it.

The Apostle Paul seems to have experienced times of spiritual dryness, too, as when he describes his inner struggles with sinful desires in Romans 7. But he persevered through difficult times. Consider what he wrote about combating feelings of discontentment:

> *I am not saying this because I am in need, for I have learned to be content whatever the circumstances. I know what it is to be in need, and I know what it is to have plenty. I have learned the secret of being content in any and every situation, whether well fed or hungry, whether living in plenty or in want.*
> *Philippians 4:11-12*

Notice that Paul said he *learned* to be content. Why should we expect it to have been any different for the faithful servants of the Parable? And why should we expect it to be any different for us? We, too, can learn to be content, even in the toughest times. We do so by being aware of our destiny. By understanding God's will. By employing the resources God in his providence has entrusted to us.

God's Presence

By gaining and applying wisdom. And by exercising initiative for God's glory.

Of course, the Parable cannot teach us everything about living productive, joyful lives that glorify God. But it is remarkably rich, and we are wise to study it again and again in the context of all God's revelation, finding new ways to apply its truths.

****

> *Do not merely listen to the word, and so deceive yourselves. Do what it says. Anyone who listens to the word but does not do what it says is like a man who looks at his face in a mirror and, after looking at himself, goes away and immediately forgets what he looks like. But the man who looks intently into the perfect law that gives freedom, and continues to do this, not forgetting what he has heard, but doing It – he will be blessed in what he does.*
>
> *James 1:22-25*

****

About the Author

Dale Schultz was born in Michigan, grew up in California, and currently lives in Delaware with his wife and two children. He received his education at the California Institute of Technology and the Massachusetts Institute of Technology. When not writing, he reads, gardens, and serves as a sales and financial consultant.

For more information, please visit the publisher's web site, www.BeechHillPress.com or send email to info@BeechHillPress.com.

www.ingramcontent.com/pod-product-compliance
Lightning Source LLC
Chambersburg PA
CBHW070521030426
42337CB00016B/2046